From Broken to Beautiful

A memoir by Peri Lynn Stitzel
Co-authored with Catherine Runyon

First printing October 20, 2018

ISBN No. 9781726235358
Published by Stitzel Enterprises
Byron Center, Michigan
In cooperation with
Golden Apple Greetings, Allendale, Mich.

CONTENTS

ACKNOWLEDGMENTS

Stitzel family photo provided
courtesy of Beth Stitzel.
Cathy Runyon's photo by Jeffrey Cunningham
Cover art suggested by grandson Johnny Galler.
References to Wedgwood Christian Services and
Christian Youth Home are used by permission.
Quotation from Dr. Andrea Brandt
used by permission.

A Little One at Risk

What happens to children who experience pain at the hands of those who should comfort and protect?

When those entrusted with their nurture and safety instead give abuse, abandonment and fear?

Can the twisted view of the world those children develop ever be made straight?

Is the broken trust ever mended?

And when they become adults, what scars remain?

Can those children ever be made whole?

When my father and stepmother began to abuse me, I was too young to cross the street by myself, too young to prepare food or bathe alone or make a telephone call. I was dependent on my parents for every aspect of my life, yet I quickly learned that they were just as likely to hurt me as to help me.

I was born in 1953 and can trace the beginnings of abuse to when I was 5. From then on, I felt frustrated and alone, though I could not put those feelings into words. I lived in constant fear, with stress and tension building year by year as the abuse intensified.

Though I could not express my feelings, I knew my home was not right. Sometimes I would visit my cousins and they had toys around that they were allowed to play with, unlike my own home. They didn't have to go to bed at their parents' convenience. Their bedrooms were a mess, but they didn't get in trouble for that. When I went to my grandma's, she gave me cakes and candy. At home, my stepmother gave those things only to my father, not to me. My grandma let me watch television and rock in her rocking chair as long as I wanted. More than the relief from discipline, it was the generosity of other people that impressed me and contrasted so sharply with the authorities in my life.

I used to play that I was a princess, living in another world. I would watch "Tarzan" on TV and pretend I was Jane and Tarzan would come to rescue me. I had make-believe worlds I could crawl into at any time. It wasn't healthy, childish imagination; I was trying to escape the real world. There was always pain and fear in my life.

Those outside my family who might have helped did not believe I was in danger. I was powerless to change my life, like a fairy tale princess locked in the dungeon needing a hero. But it would be many years until a hero appeared for me.

My earliest memories are of living happily on a farm for about two years, from the time I was about 2 until I was 4. I was surrounded by three dogs – two collie dogs called "Lassie" dogs and a small "Schnapzie" dog – and a cat named Cat. There were also two statues of black boys holding lanterns by the driveway. Both my birth parents had been previously married and had children from those marriages. When all the children were together at the farm, we were quite a group! There was a pony, and my five older siblings (three half-sisters and two half-brothers) gave me rides. I used to collect chicken eggs with the other children on the neighbor's farm. And I loved wearing hats of all shapes and sizes. My birth mother and my aunt were there, and although I don't remember him being at the farm, my father must have been there, too, from time to time. These are treasured memories, because they are the only happy ones I can recall from that time. I remember feeling love from my aunt and grandmother (my father's mother) but all was not well. My father would come home drunk and fight with my mother so bitterly that my half-brother and half-sister and I hid behind the couch in fear.

After the farm years, I have very few happy memories. What happy times that may have happened have been blotted out by the dark turn my life took.

Even before I was born, my father, mother and stepmother had developed behaviors that would affect me. My birth mother was married to another man at the time she met my father, who was divorced from his first wife. My mother had an affair with my father and I was conceived. She divorced her husband and married my father within the space of two months, and we went to live on the farm in the Detroit, Michigan area. The broken promises and relationships set the tone for my home for many years to come.

My father traveled a lot developing his business. (He owned an airplane parts manufacturing company.) My birth mother was often alone and soon started a relationship with another man. When I was about 3, I walked into the bedroom and found them in bed together. Shortly thereafter, when I was 4, my biological parents decided to divorce, and began a custody battle over me. My father sued for custody, not because he wanted me but to hurt my mother.

My mother had moved to Florida, taking me with her. My mother's older children went to live with their dad. My father's other children always lived with their mother. I was now the only child in the Florida house.

When I was four and a half, I began attending preschool. One day, my father picked me up from preschool, but instead of going home, he took me back to Michigan, an attempt at gaining custody. I wasn't afraid. He wasn't mean to me until after he married my stepmother. We went to the airport and he bought me a toy guitar. My grandmother took care of me for a while.

My parents' divorce was final before I turned five. Before their relationship ended, my birth mother emptied the bank account, and even picked the stones out of my father's rings. My father was very bitter. He had to start all over, financially, at age 44.

My father finally got custody of me because he convinced his friends to agree to sign a document stating that they had all slept with my mother. He threatened to use the document to ruin my mother's reputation if she didn't relinquish me. In the 1950s this was a much more serious threat than today, so she agreed. Little did she know that my father's vindictive nature was such that he made sure she didn't see me again for 14 years. I was essentially without a mother from age 5 until I was an adult. Though I would receive anonymously delivered packages from time to time that I later learned she had sent, I had no communication with my birth mother until I was 19.

My middle-aged father was now alone and broke with a preschooler to care for. He needed a housekeeper and someone for childcare, the driving forces behind his courtship of my stepmother, Frances, who was 27. They met at a bar. By showing her a good time and flashing some loose cash, he convinced her he was wealthy. This new wife had a career as a professional model, but now had to stay at home and take care of another woman's child when my father was traveling. She made no secret of the fact that she did not like the situation. I'm told I looked a lot like my mother. Perhaps when my stepmother looked at me, she saw the other woman, and she was jealous.

Though I missed my birth mother terribly, I was glad to have a new momma. I soon learned, however, the new mother was not like the first one.

"Don't ever call me mother again," she said to me one day. "You can call me Miss Frances or Mrs. Byard." Caring for me was too much for her. She put me to bed at 8:30 at night, and did not allow me to get up, even to go to the bathroom. Often, I wet the bed. Then she punished me, sometimes rubbing my face on the wet sheets and making me take the bedclothes to the laundry. She told me she had had five miscarriages and blamed them on me because I was so hard to take care of. She convinced my father to place me in institutional care. Shortly after I turned 5, I was sent away to St. Mary's Home in Canada, the first of several children's foster homes where I would live.

At about this same time, I was subjected to genital surgery. Like many of their generation, my stepmother and my father were preoccupied with the fear that their children would masturbate. Surgery to alter genitals of both female and male children for no medical purpose was legal and common in the United States until 1997. It was done in the hope children would not touch themselves. The surgery performed on me was called infibulation, the narrowing of the vaginal opening through the creation of a covering seal. The covering was formed by cutting and repositioning the labia minora, but without removal of the clitoris as is done in some cultures.

I had no memory of the surgery and no memory of pain. I remember having wheelchair races with other children in the hospital hallways. Later, however, there would be unforeseen consequences of this surgery.

Eleven months later, just before I turned six, I was placed in a second institution, the Children's Orthogenic School in Detroit. I lived there for nine months until the age of 6 years and 8 months. I then lived at home for two months, then at St. Mary's Academy in Detroit for nine months. I then began going to Lafayette Clinic as an outpatient, beginning in November 1961, for counseling. I don't know what the counseling was for, except that the continual moving and separation had begun to affect my behavior.

I went to Lafayette for three months, then at age 7 was sent to Devereaux Academy in Pennsylvania where I lived from January 1962 to August 1963. It was a big, old house. Girls lived on the second floor, and boys on the third floor. I left at the age of almost 10, going into the fourth grade.

I didn't go home for breaks all the time but I do remember one time I must have done so because I returned by plane alone. The staff member who was supposed to pick me up at the airport was very late. I waited, sitting near the airline agent who boarded people. A man kept coming by, offering to give me a ride, but she wouldn't let him take me. I was scared, and I was sick.

Finally, after one of my vacations, my parents did not return me to the school. I think the reason I didn't return was that my father could not, or would not, pay for it.

Invisible Abuse

Abuse takes many forms. All of them say one thing to a child: you have no value to me. The parents have total power over the child and can use him or her as they will. The abusive actions reinforce the parent's position of control and are an outlet for whatever hostilities the parent is dealing with – anger, disappointment, insecurities.

My parents and I weren't getting along well during those early years, even though I was not living at home most of the time. Nothing I did seemed to please them. I was always aware that I was unwanted by my stepmother, a fact that creates a special hurt in a child.

When I was home between stays in institutions, she would set the table for everyone for meals if her nieces or other step children were visiting. Then she would set a separate place for me at another area away from everyone else.

Once she punished me by putting me in the corner where I had to stand all day. I spit on the wall and watched it run down to the ground because I was so bored.

When I requested a doll as a gift, she bought the doll for me, but kept it wrapped in another room and wouldn't give it to me. I would sneak in when she was away, carefully unwrap it and hug it, then wrap it back up. She never gave it to me.

Sitting in the dining cove, a small eating area, was a scary experience, because quite often, without reason or warning, when my stepmother would walk behind me, she would hit me on the head with silverware she had in her hand. If crumbs fell to the floor, I was told to lick them up like a dog. I did not dare refuse.

Once my stepmother's parents came to stay with me when she and my father went on a trip. My stepmother told me that there were cameras hidden all over the house, watching me constantly and that she would look at the film when she came home. She said I would be disciplined for any wrongdoing that she saw. One night I was so scared that I was crying in my bed. My grandmother came in. She was a very gentle, soft-spoken woman. When I told her why I was crying, a great sadness filled her eyes and she told me that there were no cameras in the house.

My grandmother Martin, Frances' mother, was very special to me because in little ways, she protected me from her daughter's wrath. One holiday season, I accidentally broke the can opener.

I don't remember how, but I was terrified of what my stepmother would do when she found out. My father had used it just before that. When I told my grandmother my problem, she said she would take care of it. When my stepmother came into the kitchen, my grandmother said, "That crazy husband of yours just used the can opener and now it doesn't work." She saved my neck. I believe this woman recognized her daughter's problem.

Once I made some drawings while my parents were gone on vacation. I gave them to Grandma Martin as a gift. The drawings were not traced; I had very carefully copied them in larger form from a magazine. But when my stepmother came home, she berated me and slapped me until I "confessed" that I had traced them. It was as if I couldn't do anything good in her eyes. She would not accept anything I did.

The anguish was beginning to take a toll. One day while my stepmother and I were driving down a dirt road, I thought how wonderful it would be to just get out there, alone, and run away. Almost as if she were reading my thoughts, she stopped the car and told me to get out. When I did, she drove away while I stood alone and watched the car disappear down the road. She finally came back for me, laughing at her own cruel joke and my childish fear.

My parents sometimes left me alone with the German shepherd, Beau, as my babysitter, even though they knew (or possibly because of it) that I was deathly afraid of him. I stood on the chair in the kitchen with the dog barking at me, scared to death that he was going to kill me.

They would wake me up at night after they got back from an evening out if they found anything out of place that I had forgotten to put away. I became paranoid about going to sleep. I was afraid that if I left anything out I would be punished in the night. I would stalk the house over and over again looking for anything that wasn't perfect.

My stepmother had never wanted me near her and her cruelty took many forms. But now, in addition to her rejection, she actually began to physically abuse me, and so did my father.

Physical Abuse

My stepmother would tell my dad about something I had done or had not done, and then he would lose his temper. One day at the dinner table, she sweetly told him something about me, but the remark was designed to enrage him. He picked up a dinner plate and threw it across the table at me. It hit me in the mouth, chipped one tooth and cracked another. I remember the taste of blood mixed with mashed potatoes going down my throat with the piece of tooth. The damage was not repaired for several years.

One evening my father sent me to the kitchen to get a wooden bread serving board, then proceeded to beat me with it until it broke. Then he told me to go get another one. I obeyed, as terrorized children do, and was beaten some more.

When my father kicked me all over the face and head one night, it was my stepmother who went out in the early hours of the morning to buy medication to put on my wounds. While it seemed a kind thing to do, I never knew what to expect. One minute she could be tender, and the next, abusive.

One day she shoved my head into the toilet, splitting the skin on my forehead and holding my face under the water. I was able to get free, but the bleeding from the cut would not stop. Finally, after about an hour, I timidly asked her to help me. She cleaned my face and applied medication and a bandage so lovingly it was hard to believe it was she who had caused the injury. It was hard to comprehend she was the same person.

When my father was away, often for weeks at a time, my stepmother would be just as violent as he was. One day in winter I was going out the back door and apparently did not go quickly enough. She picked up the snow shovel from the porch and slammed it on my back.

One night when my father was away he telephoned my stepmother and, amidst a string of profanities, told her to get me out of the house before he came home. She told me to get out, and I asked where I was supposed to go. She said she didn't really care. I stayed in the house, out of my father's way. But he called me into the kitchen. He held my hands over a kettle of boiling water until they were blistered all over. Then he sent me to my room and told me to do my homework.

The day President John F. Kennedy was shot, my stepmother wanted to go shopping. My father wanted to watch the news coverage on TV and not be bothered, so he tied me to a chair in my bedroom. He threatened to send me away to a mental hospital where they would "lock me in a padded cell with a slit in the door where food would come in and out." That image haunted me for years.

Sometime during this period of my life, some of my stepmother's jewelry was stolen. I think it was my half-brother who took it, but I was blamed. I was spanked and spanked with paddles and belts until I "confessed." I said I had hidden the jewelry in the dirt in the bushes outside the front of the house. Then I spent hours digging, looking for the jewelry that I knew wasn't there. I quickly learned that telling the truth would only get me into trouble. I became a very adept little liar, something I struggled with for years afterward.

While mental abuse is difficult to see, there was also growing evidence of physical abuse if my life, yet no one asked questions about it. There were no close neighbors or children to play with. Next door was an older couple with whom we did not socialize.

I wore long sleeves to school and no one asked me about my bruises. Not surprisingly, I did not do well in school and had to have help with my work. For some time, I did not attend school at all.

I had one friend at school, named Norma, who understood I was unhappy at home. One day I had to stay after school for some reason. Norma believed I would get in trouble if I didn't go right home. She stayed at school in my place. I have always been thankful in my heart for her.

I did not have the benefit of a close church family. Sometimes I went to the Catholic church with my stepmother and my father where I learned about prayer. I didn't have a rosary, so I used my fingers and toes to pray the rosary at night, begging God not to let me wake up the next day. Then, when I did wake up, I was very disappointed.

Though I was only about 10, I had begun to think about ending my own life. I once tried swallowing a bunch of aspirin, but nothing happened. I also ate what I thought were poisonous berries that grew on bushes in front of the house. My stepmother once showed me a gun that was kept in the house and told me I could use it to kill myself if I wanted to.

There was nowhere to escape except outdoors. In the summer, I stayed outdoors by the hour, weeding our extremely large lawn, just to stay out of my stepmother's way. The yard was so big that, by the time I finished weeding the front yard, the weeds in back had started growing again.

Abandonment and Loneliness

I am not sure exactly when the physical violence against me first started, because by the time I was 13, I had been in six different youth facilities and dates were lost to me. Physical violence seemed to erupt every time I was at home between the various locations.

One place I lived was a Catholic facility. It was an orphanage. I was supposed to be there for two weeks while my stepmother had surgery. I stayed for two years. I remember the grounds seemed to go on forever, and I played with a friend who had me convinced that trees were real beings and we had to be kind to them or they could hurt us. There also were wonderful nuns that were so sweet I wanted to grow up to be one. I also noticed they wore layers and layers of clothing. I liked that. It would protect me from being touched or hurt.

The succession of institutions kept me away from my stepmother and father for most of my early years – St. Mary's in Canada, St. Mary's in Detroit, Lafayette, St. Vincent DePaul, Deveraux, St.

Vincent and Sarah Fisher Center, Kingswood private mental hospital, and finally, when I was 13, Christian Youth Homes in Grand Rapids (now Wedgwood Christian Services).

But between stints at various facilities, I lived with my father and stepmother. Knowing I was unwanted at home was punishment in itself but going home was also a threat as I suffered first rejection and neglect and later physical and sexual abuse whenever I was there. Eventually, my parents would find a new location to treat what they called my behavior and mental problems and I was shipped out once more.

I was at the Sarah Fisher home for about a year. I remember the day that they told me I was going home. They acted happy for me, but I cried. They had no idea what they were sending me back to. I wanted to stay there. It felt safe, but children had no say in those days, so I was returned to my home.

You may be wondering, Why was I sent away to all these children's homes? Was there something wrong with me that I'm not telling you? No, there wasn't anything wrong with me in the beginning, except that I was a young child who missed her mommy and didn't understand why I couldn't see her. I believe I was sent away because I wasn't wanted by my stepmother. My father, in trying to hang onto this, his third marriage, agreed to send me away. As the years went by and the abuse cut into my soul as well as my body, then yes, I did have problems. I was disobedient and lied and had problems that I couldn't talk about because no one would listen.

I prayed for death nightly and was angry at God when I awakened the next day in the same environment. I read books whenever I could, because only there did I find a world untouched by the terror I was experiencing. There I found happy endings and often reread them – *Heidi* was a favorite – clinging, I suppose to the hope of someday being rescued myself.

I dearly loved my Grandpa Cecil (top left) but would be shut off from him after my biological parents divorced. At right, I model one of my more daring hats at about age five. Above, I was reunited with Dick Gritter, founder and director of Wedgwood Christian Services for 35 years; and Molly Guilliaume, who nurtured me while I lived there.

Sexual Abuse

When I was 11 years old, my stepmother's abuse took on a new dimension. She had accused me of masturbating throughout my early life. I had no idea what she was talking about. I do remember having an infection that included itching, but my actions were not sexual in nature. Now, as I approached adolescence, her accusations were more intense. She had been on rages before and I figured this one would pass, too. This was when the physical abuse took on a sexual element.

My body was beginning to develop, but she claimed it was unnatural. She began a daily regimen of trying to mutilate me. Once she bound my chest with Ace bandages wrapped so tightly they cut into my skin. I still have a scar from that. She used sandpaper on my budding breasts, then smeared the raw skin with Vicks, the stinging medication adding to the pain. I had to go to school with bindings on my chest. All the other girls were wearing training bras, but I had to wear undershirts. We were supposed to shower after gym, but I refused because I was so embarrassed. Because of this, I failed gym. My father was terribly angry, but I was too embarrassed to tell him the real reason for the failing grade.

I was growing up, but I was still afraid of my stepmother. She threatened me with physical harm if I did not obey her when she told me to lie down on the bed. Then she inserted pencils and similar objects into my vagina. Her treatment was so rough I suffered bruising and swelling in the genital area.

Because of the surgery performed when I was 5, my vaginal opening was too small to accommodate normal menstrual flow. When my periods started, they were terribly painful.

I begged my parents to believe I wasn't touching myself, as they had accused. I asked my father to tie me to the bed at night with my hands tied to the bed posts so I could prove to them that I wasn't doing it.

My dad, through all this time, never knew of any of the sexual abuse; my stepmother only did it when he was gone.

As I grew older, I discerned more of my stepmother's character, though I did not understand it. Once I tried to fight back against her. I was on one side of the bed and she was on the other, screaming obscenities at me, when the telephone rang. She left the room to answer it and in a mature, polite, calm voice, she said, "Hello, Byard residence, can I help you?" I was so shocked! I thought she must be insane. She had gone from a screaming maniac to a sophisticated lady in a moment.

I noticed that she never hurt me when she had her makeup on, only when her face was plain. It was as if she turned into the gracious lady whenever she was dressed up to go out.

My dad was making good money at this time. Frances was wearing furs and mink coats and they belonged to the local country club. Still, they often fought between themselves. My dad knocked her around quite a bit. They broke a number of ash trays in their angry exchanges, and a couple of lamps.

I believe there were deeper problems between my father and his wife, and he began trying to stay apart from her. I lived with my father in Florida for six months the year I was 12. She only visited once during that time that I can recall. Those were the best six months of my childhood after my father married my stepmother. Those were the safest and the least stressful months. My father was different there. He was calmer and never hit me or lost his temper.

There was an incident when I was stealing from him. I took quarters I found in his dresser drawers. I had been introduced to pornographic magazines by an older girl at school at that time and wanted money to buy them. I felt for sure I would get a beating for stealing (I hid the magazines and never told him about them), but instead, he sat quietly on my bed and told me how disappointed he was in me. It was then that I had a glimpse of the man my dad could be. However, that glimpse faded when I had to return to live with my stepmother in June 1965.

By December of 1966, at age 13, I had become so nervous and dysfunctional I was sent to see a psychiatrist. The sexual and physical abuse were getting worse all the time. The doctor prescribed large doses of Thorazine to calm my nerves. At this time, I couldn't talk to him and tell him what was going on in my home because I was afraid of retribution. Once when I was at camp in the summer, I told the staff what was going on in my home. Instead of reaching out to help me they packed up my belongings and shipped me back home that same night, telling my stepmother that I was telling the most awful stories ever imagined.

One day after a particularly bad night I saw the psychiatrist, in his office. I found the courage to tell him a little of what was going on in my home, though my stepmother sat nearby in the waiting room. As usual, the doctor talked to my stepmother after he talked to me. When we went home that night, she didn't lay a hand on me, and for the next six nights she didn't touch me. I knew something was going on, but I didn't know what.

I didn't know it then, but God was intervening. It was as if He said to Satan, "Enough! She cannot handle any more. I will open this man's eyes to see what she cannot fully express." Unknown to me, this doctor believed me, and was about to have me put in a place of safety, even though I wouldn't see it as that. That evening there was no abuse. Then all week, no abuse. I knew something was going on but I had learned by then to keep my mouth shut. I would find out soon enough.

One week later, in January 1967, when I was in the eighth grade, I came home from school one day and found my stepmother had dinner ready for me at four o'clock in the afternoon. I remember It was a Swanson TV dinner. While I was eating, she called to me from another room, asking me where I was keeping the skirt I was making in sewing class, and where my toothbrush was. I knew she was planning something. I soon learned she had a suitcase packed and after I finished my dinner, we got my coat and got in the car. It wasn't until I was almost there that she told me she was taking me to a private mental hospital, which the psychiatrist had recommended. I was so scared! My father's warning came to my mind. I had visions of spending the rest of my life in pajamas in a padded room with my food coming through a slit in the locked door. I didn't know what I feared more – home or the hospital.

I remember checking in, hearing the clanging of each door we passed through and how it would electronically lock behind us. I was the only child in the hospital. The next oldest person was 25 years old.

After my stepmother left, I asked the nurses if I could keep my clothes on and they smiled and said yes. They told me the only time I would be locked in my room would be if I got violent. It was such a relief. I could move around. I could watch TV. I could relax, and nobody there would harm me. They had books for me to read and arts and crafts to do. To me, it was like heaven. I wanted to just stay there forever.

When I got there, I had a complete physical examination. Years later, I realized that was probably why my stepmother stopped hurting me. She was trying to allow enough time to pass to let the bruises fade before I got to the hospital. But there was enough evidence beneath my clothing to convince the doctor that I was in trouble.

I found a nurse that was easy to talk to and told her my story. She in turn told the doctor for me. However, the documentation of abuse somehow was lost when I left the hospital. I would not receive any counseling about the sexual abuse.

I was at Kingswood private mental hospital in Pontiac, Michigan for six months. I was heavily medicated, though I don't know why. I didn't misbehave at home, and certainly did not misbehave at this hospital. I was so heavily medicated, I would sometimes fall asleep sitting up. I was excused from arts and crafts because I couldn't function. I remember the time my parents, who then lived in nearby Royal Oak, came to take me for the evening, which might have been Easter. I slept all day so I could stay awake from 6 to 9 p.m., the amount of time I was to be out.

The nurse continued to be very caring and I found myself able to open up to her and confide my nightmare. She related it all to the doctor and he in turn arranged a social worker to help me. By now I was emotionally hurt and needed a safe place to go where I would not be afraid. I was so constantly tense, afraid that my parents would come and take me, that I had to be medicated so I could relax. A case worker was assigned to me. She was to find another home for me to live in which would be far enough away from Detroit that I wouldn't fear running into my family on the street. She did find a home for emotionally disturbed girls. It was in Grand Rapids, called Christian Youth Homes (Now Wedgwood Christian Services).

Healing Begins

On June 12, 1967, a Wednesday at 1 o'clock in the afternoon, I came to live at that home. This was the first time in all the homes I had been that the staff members were not only Christian but dedicated, openly practicing Protestants.

One staff member at Wedgwood wore a cross on a chain around her neck. I noticed there was no figure of Jesus on the cross as I had seen in the Catholic facilities. I asked her where the Jesus figure was. She told me that Christ had died but had risen; He was no longer on the cross, a cause for joy. While I knew that Jesus had risen, it was a new idea for me that His life could affect behavior.

For the next year, I observed their Christianity. There was never a staff member that touched me, although I got plenty of work detail for bad behavior. I would slam doors in their faces, swear and have screaming outrages, but they continued to stay calm. Some of my bad behavior was because of my fear and anxiety, but some was simply testing them to see how far I could go.

I was very, very lonely when I arrived at Wedgwood. I used to follow the housemother everywhere. She told me later that I reminded her of a puppy dog. I wanted someone to love me so badly, and I didn't know how to get that love. I was so eager for friendship that I turned some of the girls off by being too aggressive. I didn't know how to act in that type of social setting. I wouldn't trust anybody.

Molly Guiliaume was among the staff members who formed a strong relationship with me. "I was young when she was my patient," Guillaume remembers. "I took her to the dentist. They had her get in the chair and she started screaming. The assistant called me in to be with her during the procedure. She finally made it through the appointment. The reason she was so upset was related to the abuse she had.

"I would rate the abuse quite high. She would tell me about life in the Detroit area, about the long hedge around her house where she spent hours. She made up fantasy stories about the flowers, going into another world to survive the day.

"Kids who come into care usually do a lot of testing (of boundaries) because they don't trust anyone. Peri had never been placed anywhere very pleasant. It was hard for her to learn to accept love and sincere caring, hard for her to believe it was real. That took a lot of time."

At that time, I could still withdraw into a fantasy world. I especially liked being Maid Marian in the Robinhood stories. After counseling with Molly Guillaume, I accepted that I had to live in the world I was in.

The average stay for young people at Wedgwood was about nine months. I stayed four years. My first days at Wedgwood were filled with learning how to live with 12 other girls, learning the rules and getting to know the staff. As I grew more relaxed, my deeper problems began to emerge. Without the threat of being hit, all my inner turmoil began to erupt – temper outbursts, anger, swearing, disobedience, aggressive and manipulative actions, all of which resulted in being grounded.

Through it all, I continued to observe the staff's lifestyles – in essence, their Christianity in action. It became evident to me that whatever or whoever they believed in was obviously different than the past experiences I'd had with people who called themselves Christians and who had even gone to church.

31

Throughout the first year of my stay, I began to experience love and a caring relationship with these people that I had never known before. No matter how disobedient I was, there was never any physical retaliation.

Love Steps In

The following summer, 1968, I was sent to Grace Youth Camp in Mears, Michigan with the other girls. On June 13, on a Saturday evening, we had a chapel speaker who talked about heaven and hell, and for the first time in my life, I realized that I was separated from God and going to hell.

The speaker talked about Jesus, who had suffered for me. As I sat there listening, I compared what he had gone through with my own abuse. A crown of thorns had been forced onto his head; my head had been slashed and bruised when thrust into a toilet. He suffered whipping by the Roman soldiers; I had been beaten with a bread board and belts by my father. His hands were pierced by nails; my own hands were blistered in steam.

I couldn't imagine anyone going through that for me. I knew I would never go through that for anyone else, so when I realized that Jesus had gone through everything I had gone through – even dying – because He loved me, I accepted Him as my personal savior. Two friends assisted me in my

33

decision. We were beside the camp fire at night, with just the heat of the fire to warm us, as I prayed, confessing my sin, thanking Him for His sacrifice and accepting His gift of salvation.

I remember thinking that if He went through all that for me and died for me, then I wanted Him for my savior. If someone had said God loved me like a father, I would have told them where to go and how to get there, but I connected very personally with the pain Christ suffered for me.

It almost didn't happen. About six weeks before my salvation, staff members at Wedgwood had a meeting to discuss my treatment and felt they could offer me no more help. I was under the impression that they seriously considered sending me to the state mental facility, sort of the end of the line. If I had gone there, I would probably still be there. One staff member, an older woman, fought for me and asked them to give me one more chance. Then I met Jesus Christ. I believe it was this supernatural rebirth that made it possible for me to begin the healing process in my life.

I am told that the change in my life was so immediate that the staff knew something had happened to me. I was still taking 250 mg of Thorazine. I still had my problems, but as I had read in a book called *I never Promised You a Rose*

Garden, (Hannah Green, 1964, Holt, Henry and Company), healing takes time. I knew that Jesus hadn't promised me instant healing. What He had promised me was His salvation, and we could work it all out together and the healing in my life would come in time. I know there were many people who cared for me over the years who meant well, but I needed more than a change in behavior. I needed a new heart, which only new life in Christ could bring.

The night of my salvation I was reading that book. I had it in my back pack and God spoke to my heart. I felt Him speak, saying "I'm not promising you a rose garden, but you will get better over time and I will be with you."

There were many who cared for me. They showed me how to do things to make other people feel better. They explained when I did something wrong (once I ran away, for a couple of hours). I began getting off medication. I wrote a letter to my father. I had my ups and downs, but I felt a difference inside. I wasn't alone anymore.

I returned to Wedgwood after camp, working all the problems through one day at a time. The next three years passed quickly and I began to learn about normal life. I went to school. I even had a boyfriend and a few dates. I watched staff, often learning from their examples how I wanted to grow up. I used to spend hours in conversation with staff, sharing wounds that needed airing in order to be healed, talking about their lives in order to help me make decisions on how to live mine. Jesus was very important to them and so He became important to me.

The next three years also brought high school life. The ups and downs that I struggled through in the adolescent years were like most everybody else. The doctors slowly decreased my medication and I remember once throwing it away for three weeks to prove to the staff that I could handle myself without tranquilizers. They didn't know I had thrown it away until I told them. At that point workers contacted the psychiatrist and recommended that I be taken off the medication. He agreed, saying it should be given only if I asked for it. I took it two more times, when I was extremely upset from a family situation.

Sometime after I made the decision to accept salvation and got off medication, when I was about 16, I tried to share my newfound faith in a letter to my father. His response was a letter to me filled with profanity. He said that what was making me better was his money and that God had nothing to with it.

My senior year in high school, my parents were going to pull me out of Wedgwood (I was attending a Grand Rapids High School) and put me in a private academy, a finishing school, so they could tell their friends I had graduated from a prestigious school and introduce me to their society. I wanted nothing to do with it. I was scared and begged my caseworker to make them keep me at Wedgwood. I threatened to run away, even throw rocks through a police car window to be put into custody. I would have done anything to keep from going with my father and stepmother. God showed His might. He worked through my caseworker.

At that time, I had a job at a local retail store in a special program for young women. I got my boss to schedule me to work the day before and the day after Christmas, so I used that flimsy excuse as the reason I could not go home for the holidays. My parents saw right through it. My father called and said I had better have my bags packed because he was coming to pull me out of the home. When he arrived, a staff member sent him to the office across the street – for three hours! My caseworker very diplomatically handled my father. When I was called to see him, I was told I could stay at Wedgwood, but my father would only pay the minimum. My job would have to pay for clothes and anything else I required.

I know God worked mightily that day, because my father was not a man to be manipulated by anyone when he set his mind to something.

Maturing in Faith

As I progressed in my faith, I learned to accept others and care about them, understanding that others had problems, too.

At my graduation ceremony, a student jumped off the podium and ran out a side door. Police were waiting for him and arrested him because he was high on drugs. I ran into him years later at a church. He told me, "All the time I was in jail, I kept remembering you carrying a Bible in school."

I had carried the Bible to school but I was scared about doing it. People teased me, but I kept carrying it.

The man said, "I couldn't figure out what was so important about that. I decided to read the Bible to find out, and I got saved." I saw that God could use me in the lives of others.

Childhood abuse affected my social relationships through high school and young adulthood. I was ignorant of sexual behavior and responses and didn't know what was normal, such as a kiss after a date, or what was happening to me when I was sexually aroused. I missed out on having close girlfriends because of my living arrangements.

I was comforted in that time by my relationship with Christ. Though I missed out on human relationships during my teen years, I took refuge in my salvation and the promise of heaven. Later, God would bring people into my life who met the human need for companionship and family love.

When I graduated from high school, the time had come to leave Wedgwood and be on my own. Wedgwood helped me to get a job and find a place to live. I left there physically strong, with a faith I'd never lose, having met the only God who could heal my mind and restore my joy.

On Tuesday, June 15, 1971, at 4:30 p.m., I moved out of Wedgwood and began life on my own. There was a boarding house called Elmcrest for single young women at 221 Jones St. in Grand Rapids. I lived there for the summer, working two jobs, both part-time, and staying out of trouble. At the beginning of August, I woke up one morning with a severe stomach ache. I called my doctor who sent me to Butterworth Hospital (now Spectrum Health) to be examined. Because no one at Elmcrest thought I looked sick, I could not get a ride, so I walked to the hospital with my purse clutched to my stomach. I was diagnosed with appendicitis. Because I was only 17, the hospital called my father to get permission to operate. He was at the golf course, the same course and on the same hole as when he was called about the death of his mother. He gave permission and they operated.

My father flew up from Florida where he was living then to see me. He was so gentle and kind. Most of the Wedgwood staff members that I knew were on vacation at that time so I had the office secretary at my side for comfort. My father told me to call my stepmother. She was very concerned, he said, so when I was strong enough, I walked down to the pay telephone and called her.

My stepmother accused me of faking the illness and said I should have had a second opinion. She continued on and on. I was so upset that I just cried and cried. Nurses had to help me back to my room. My pastor and his wife took me home with them for my recuperation time because I could not go down steps at the boarding house. My father called my pastor and demanded that he put me on a bus and send me to the house in Detroit as soon as I was well enough. My pastor told me that, for the first time in his life, he would counsel me not to obey my parents.

I had wanted to attend Grace Bible College in Wyoming, Michigan, but I had no funds. I had applied for a loan or student grant, but my request was denied. The authorities at the school were afraid to go against my parent's wishes, which they knew about because my pastor knew my situation and he was an official at the college. Two different men in my church heard about my circumstances and why I wasn't going to college. After prayer, they decided God would have them pay my way the first year, so I was able to attend. They would eventually pay for the rest of my time there as well.

That first year of college was truly a lesson to me in God's caring. I had no winter coat; someone gave a me a brand new winter coat for Christmas. Money would come in the mail from anonymous donors for my needs. Jobs seemed to fall into my lap. My needs were constantly provided.

About this time, I was also able to locate my birth mother, from whom I had been separated for 14 years. I desperately wanted that part of my life to be complete. I had so many questions and so many gaps in my memory and experience that only she could fill.

I met a wonderful friend named Dan Swanson and one Monday morning he took me to Detroit with him when he had to register for the draft. He went his way, and his mother took me to where the divorce records were kept in Pontiac, Michigan. For the next three hours I read the details of my birth parent's divorce, looking for an address or clue of where she might be. I found three addresses, two of hers, and one of my grandparents. I was very disheartened, because I knew the addresses were 14 years old and I had been led to believe that my grandparents were dead.

We went back to Dan's home and I looked up the address for my grandparents in a phone book. My whole body seemed to turn to ice when my eyes fell on their name in the book. I picked up the phone and dialed the number. A very old woman answered. I asked her if she had a daughter by the name of Mary Margaret (my mother's name). She said to me, "Mary Margaret who?" I said I didn't know her last name. She told me she did have a daughter by that name. Then I said to her, "Grandma, this is Peri Lynn." She screamed. She couldn't believe it. She asked me to come to her home.

Dan was as excited as I was. He drove me to her home in Birmingham, a suburb near Detroit. When we got there, I knocked on the door and she let me in. For the first time in 14 years, I saw my grandmother. After the crying and tears had stopped, she told me that her husband had died four months before. If I had come sooner, I would have met him. She told me how much she loved me and how they had never moved, hoping that someday I might come home and find them.

Then a young girl came out of another room. "You don't know me, but I am your sister-in-law, Jan," she said. I thought, how could I have a sister-in-law? I don't have a brother. Then I remembered I did have a half-brother, Bill, and two half-sisters from my mother's first marriage. Bill came in soon. These were the children I remembered from so long ago who had played with me on the farm. After my father's divorce from my birth mother, he had barred all contact with them, along with my mother.

It was a joyful reunion. My brother told me stories of how he used to go up to the house in Detroit when he was 16, pretending he was lost and asking for directions, but really looking for evidence of me. One of my half-sisters came down from Ann Arbor and I talked to the other half-sister in Colorado. My grandmother told me that my mother was living in Mexico with her husband and we could call her.

Grandmother called first and said, "Peg (my mother's nickname), there is someone here who wants to talk to you." She handed me the phone. I said, "Mother, this is Peri Lynn." She was as amazed as my grandmother had been. As we talked, the love in her voice overwhelmed me and I finally felt like a whole person. Six weeks later I flew to Mexico and was reunited with my mother. We spent 10 days together rebuilding our ties and afterward remained friends.

Many years later, my birth mother came to live near me in Michigan. She had many mental, social and spiritual issues to deal with. She was an atheist and hated that I was a Christian. We were not able to be close as she got older. She moved away and was well cared for by my half-brother until she died.

Molly Guillaume noted, "There were a lot of self-centered adults in Peri's life. I can't judge but they didn't give her any of the nurture that she needed. They made choices in their relationships and she was the brunt of them. I do think Peri, when she was younger, was a little pushy, somewhat controlling, and in a way kind of rigid, but she had good reason for any control issues. You have to find some way to control things in your life. The exciting thing, if you are a Christian, you have a way to deal with it."

I spent two more years at Grace Bible College, working all the while, and graduated in 1974 with an Associate of Arts degree. I spent the next year paying off my debts, working as a cashier at Food City in Wyoming, Michigan.

In August 1974, I met the man whom God had prepared for me to marry, also a student at Grace Bible College. His name is John Mark Stitzel. We dated until June 1975 and then were married.

The previous December, John had told my father and stepmother of our engagement. They wanted us to wait a year and have a big Christmas holiday-themed wedding, which they would pay for. We wanted to get married in August but when John's brother planned his wedding for August, we moved our date to June. Also, we wanted to have the summer together before returning to school in the fall. My parents refused to come to the wedding because they were going to an air show in France. They sent no gift and no one else from my stepmother's side of the family dared to come for fear of my father.

During our courtship, I told John about the abuses of my childhood. He was very understanding but I would find the injuries of the past would continue to affect me. I saw a medical doctor for a pre-marital exam before our wedding. At that time the doctor told me it was a good thing I never tried to have intercourse. He said the surgery performed when I was 5 had made the vaginal opening too small, and that was the reason I had suffered painful menstrual periods. He performed the minor surgery to widen the vaginal opening.

Though John was kind and patient, I hated the physical demonstrations of love and affection that came with marriage. I hated sexual acts and hated being touched on my breasts. I had no idea my past injuries had affected me so deeply until I was actually in the situation. Yet through God's grace and John's love and patience, we had a fulfilling relationship. In April 1977 we had our first child, a boy we named John Mark, Jr., and in June 1979 our daughter Sarah was born. God has richly blessed me with a caring husband who loves the Lord, and with two healthy children. After my father died, and as soon as my children were old enough, I told them as much about my life as they could handle.

John came into our marriage from a verbally abusive home. John had become a Christian when he was a teenager. He made the decision to leave the Catholic church he had been part of all his life and went to Grace Bible College where he studied to become a pastor. His family could not understand or accept his decision. He was rejected and told he was on his own. John met me when he came to Grace Bible College.

"In my opinion, I was damaged goods," John said, "and I was a new Christian. When I met Peri, she had been a Christian for a comparatively long time. She told me about her history. I didn't know about doctrine; I just knew God made broken people well. I thought, We can get through this.

"When I met Frances and Perry Byard, Frances said, 'If you play your cards right, you could be the son that Perry lost (through death)." She was implying financial gain. The idea was offensive to me. My interest was in Peri, not business," John said.

"After we were married, Peri's dad called. He told me, 'You're married now and you're stuck with her.' I said, 'I'm sorry you feel that way.'"

We went through some pre-marriage counseling with our pastor. In the third session, John revealed, "When I would tell her I love her, she would say, 'Do you mean that?' That made me wonder if I did. I had been formerly engaged, but then I fell in love with Peri. Could that happen again? There was tension in my heart and mind and no one to talk to. I broke up with Peri."

I was devastated. We met to talk, and John opened his heart about his previous romance. I wanted to know if he was just on the rebound. Both of us knew we wanted marriage to be for a lifetime.

We started over and John reaffirmed his love for me. Then we could begin to build trust. We shared activities, read scripture together, prayed together, attended church, and had long conversations, including talking about life issues and our differences.

"On our honeymoon, I was all excited," John said. "I got into the room, and I wanted to experience the joy of marriage, but I was trying to be patient. I said 'So, you want to go to bed, or go out to eat?' Peri immediately said she wanted to go out. When we came back from the restaurant, she was nervous. as a bride would be, but everything went well."

Our sex life was up and down. Sometimes at night when we would be sleeping and John's arm would fall across me, I would wake up screaming. I can't stand to be touched on my chest. John has had to sort through feelings of being robbed of some sexual gratification. Over the years, John has often said to me that there are lots of ways to show love besides the physical aspect but I'm sad that I haven't been able to provide all that he would enjoy because of the damage that was done to me.

Adjustments to expectations of physical satisfaction were not the only problems we faced as newlyweds.

"We had hellacious rows," John said, something he had experienced often in his childhood home. Peri could be stubborn and demanding. John yelled and once broke a door in anger. But while John had defied his father and broken that relationship, he wanted permanence in his marriage as taught in scripture. He had seen the effects of fighting between his parents, which sometimes included physical force. He was also deeply affected when a cousin's marriage finally dissolved over the cousin's insistence on going to hunting camp. "When you get married, you have to learn to mesh," he said. "Choose your battles."

Childhood abuse carried over into our parenting style. I wasn't able to breast feed my babies and I missed that. As they grew up, I made the mistake of going overboard to show affection and bought them a lot of presents. I would pay off the credit card for a year after buying anything they wanted for Christmas. That created a problem I didn't recognize until years later. I gave in to them more than I should have. But I never hit them. When I was angry or frustrated with them, I went to God for strength.

My father died at Christmas time, 1976. My stepmother, about 20 years younger than my father, continued to live on. We had no further contact. When I heard she was dead in 2015, I felt such relief and freedom. She was not going to be calling again.

On her blog, Dr. Andrea Brandt writes for "Psychology Today" about childhood abuse, "Whether you witnessed or experienced violence as a child or your caretakers emotionally or physically neglected you, when you grow up in a traumatizing environment you are likely to still show signs of that trauma as an adult.

"Children make meaning out of the events they witness and the things that happen to them, and they create an internal map of how the world is. This meaning-making helps them cope. But if children don't create a new internal map as they grow up, their old way of interpreting the world can damage their ability to function as adults." (https://www.psychologytoday.com/blog/mindful -anger/201706/4-ways-childhood-emotional- trauma-impacts-us- adults?utm_source=FacebookPost&utm_medium =FBPost&utm_campaign=FBPost).

Finding salvation in Jesus Christ was the foundation of a new "internal map" for me as I grew into adulthood and through my adult years, just as it was for John. I needed the love of Jesus to fill the void. While many well-meaning people tried to change my behavior, my supernatural experience with Christ changed my heart. Then, working through the abuse and the failed relationships as we grew in understanding of scripture provided the guidance for life.

Jesus told his followers that if anyone offended a child, it would be better if they were cast into the sea with a millstone hung around their neck (Matthew 18:6). When I read about children who have died as a result of the abuse they went through, I am not so much saddened as glad because they have been set free from a lifetime of emotional pain, nightmares, and flashbacks. And how do I feel about the captured abuser? The sentence needs to be much stiffer than it is, because once out of prison, they can pick up and begin to live life again, unlike the victim who survives. That child never gets a time where they are finally free of their past. They have to fight to have a life, for the rest of their life. They are not set free after the counseling sessions have concluded; their past will always intertwine with their present.

Though I am healed of bitterness and hatred through the love of Christ, memories of abuse abound and remain a challenge I must continually face. I was broken by abuse and neglect, yet by God' grace, I have a beautiful life in Christ, filled with love from friends and family and fellow believers.

I am who I am today by the grace of God. If the men and women of Wedgwood had not allowed Jesus to be the Lord of their life, then I would never have caught a glimpse of the savior in human form. Because of their ministry in my life, I was able to reach out and cling to the cross as my last hope. Jesus, who was wounded for me, in turn wrapped his resurrected arms around me, and has never let me go. I still have some problems but from the time I accepted Christ as savior, I knew there was Someone inside me, promising that He'd always be there every step of the way.

These past years I have suffered a great deal of physical pain from my back involving three failed operations on discs, probably related to the physical assaults in my early childhood. It has been a time of growing closer to God and learning how much He cares for me. I still have pain that I live with from day to day but that is bearable because someday it will be gone when my Lord gives me a perfect body.

People often question why God allows suffering in the world, especially for children who are too young to have made bad choices. Simply put, sin has consequences that fall in a circle wider than the sinner. For me, suffering began when my birth parents made bad choices, ignoring their promise to love their spouses and be faithful to their vows, and when my stepmother indulged her own anger and hatred instead of protecting and nurturing me.

In His time, God rescued me. I was wounded, but because of that, I love Him more. I hope my story is a testimony to His never-ending love and that it will bring hope to all who are in pain.

About the Authors

PERI STITZEL'S BEAUTIFUL LIFE includes John, her husband of 43 years; and children John Mark, his wife Beth and their daughters Lydia, Addy, Caela and Hailey; and Sara Leah (Galler), her husband Mark and their children Jade, Johnny, Silas, Shawn, Mary and Nora.

Peri has an Associate of Arts degree from Grace Bible College in Wyoming, Mich. She operated a licensed daycare in her home for 23 years and worked for several years as a community news reporter for the Advance Newspaper, now part of the MLive.com media group.

Peri has been a guest speaker for

Wedgwood Family Services, and she and John were involved with Wedgwood's Big Sister Program.

Peri enjoys gardening, studying God's Word, amateur photography, her pets and reading. She loves to travel, once winning an all-expense trip to a resort in Moab, Utah, and she once took a two-week tour of Alaska, a surprise gift from her birth mother.

In 1985 a unique presentation of her life was presented in audio form by the radio program "Unshackled" produced by Pacific Garden Mission in Chicago, entitled "Lynn", episode #1810. Her story also was featured in "Power for Living", a Sunday school take-home paper produced by Standard Publishing.

"My motivation for a book at this time is two-fold," Peri said. "I feel safe to tell the story now that my father and step-mother are both dead. I also wanted to tell my story so if I can reach even one girl who doesn't see herself as having a future, or having anything to look forward to, to tell her that yes, there is a future for her, one found in Jesus. He wants to wrap his arms around her and tell her how sorry He is for what she has been thru, and that it is not the end of her story. Her life can be restored in him, and I am proof positive of this!"

Today Peri and John and Peri's two Yorkies live in a retirement community in Kentwood, Michigan and fellowship with other believers at Byron Center Bible Church.

 **CATHERINE RUNYON** (Cathy) is a resident of Allendale, Mich. She has been writing for publication since 1971. She has written books published by Moody Publishers and Barbour and Company, and stories and interviews for Union Gospel Press, Light and Life Evangel, "Virtue" Magazine, "Woman's World" and others. She is the author of an award-winning weekly column for MLive.com (Advance Newspapers) called "Mother Lode" and works as a content producer for MLive.com. She and her husband, Randy, have been married for 50 years, and have two boys, David (Jenette) and Ed (Amy) and four grandchildren.